Iterations

Also available by **Terry Wright**
from **Redacted Skyline Press**:

Lord of the Flies Org Chart

Iterations

Art and Poetry

Terry Wright

Redacted Skyline Press
Little Rock, Arkansas
redactedskylinepress@gmail.com

ISBN (Harcover): 979-8-9912650-0-3
ISBN (Paperback): 979-8-9912650-1-0

All poems and visual art in this collection
are the work of Terry Wright.
(Instagram: @terrywrightart)

Book and Cover Design: H. K. Stewart

Printed in the United States of America

For Cindy,
who holds the pencil to the music

Google is a global Rorschach test. We see in it what we want to see.

— John Battelle

Contents

Obama Iterations

Trump Iterations

Methodology

The poems in this book are from a series called *Google Poems*. I first create an original artwork and title it. The title, now also the title of the poem, is typed into the Google Search Engine and searched. The corresponding poem is then composed by sometimes collaging the resulting prose fragments and by sometimes using material found in the links. During this process, the content of potential material becomes exponentially less heuristic and more surreal as a given search expands.

Acknowledgments

Grateful acknowledgment is made to the following places where poems and artworks in this collection have appeared:

Media: *Really System*, *Sliver of Stone*, *Spank the Carp*, *The Idle Class*, and *The New Verse News*.

Music: *Iterations*. Four Pieces for Oboe and Piano. Music by Daniel De Togni. Text by Terry Wright.

Radio/Podcast: *Iterations*. "Arts and Letters." 89.1 KUAR–FM, Little Rock Public Radio. Produced by J. Bradley Minnick.

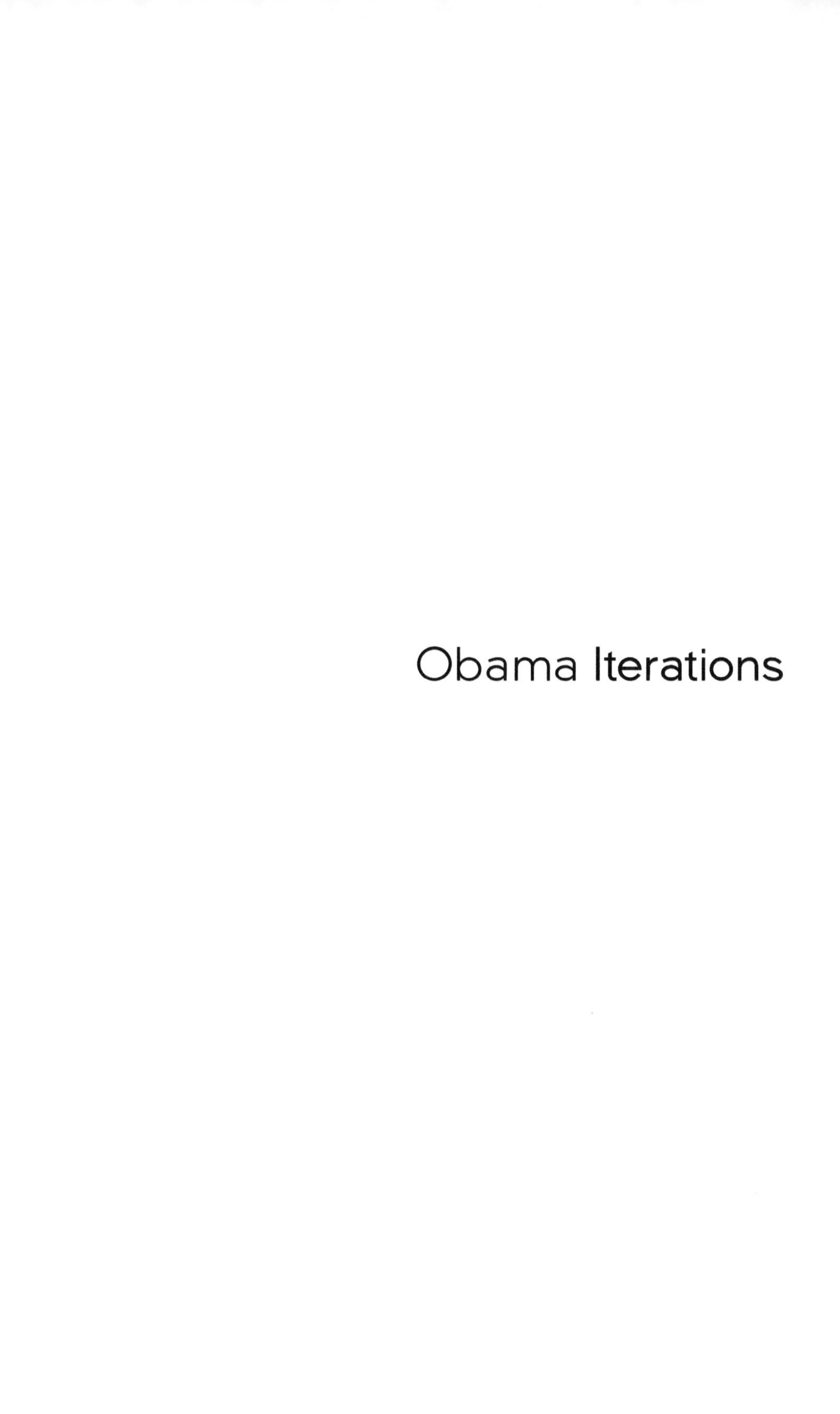

Obama Iterations

*How hard can that be? Saying that
Nazis are bad.*

— Barack Obama

At the Beach

Abusive algae bloom into a pasquinade.
Building industries nag and gnaw away horizons.

Floral umbrellas stuck in grit near a surf shop
wilt when plucked by an emergent cloudburst.

Bodies buffed to driftwood luster float by
as bagged cell phones buzz like sand flies.

Another loony family spends a week together
intimately   stressed.

Bickering and intense freckling break out
before a lifelessness cloaks like sun screen

then divorce gales blow in all   Mediterranean.
Sand castles belatedly dilapidate.

Stingrays singing under air mattresses
size up the kids.

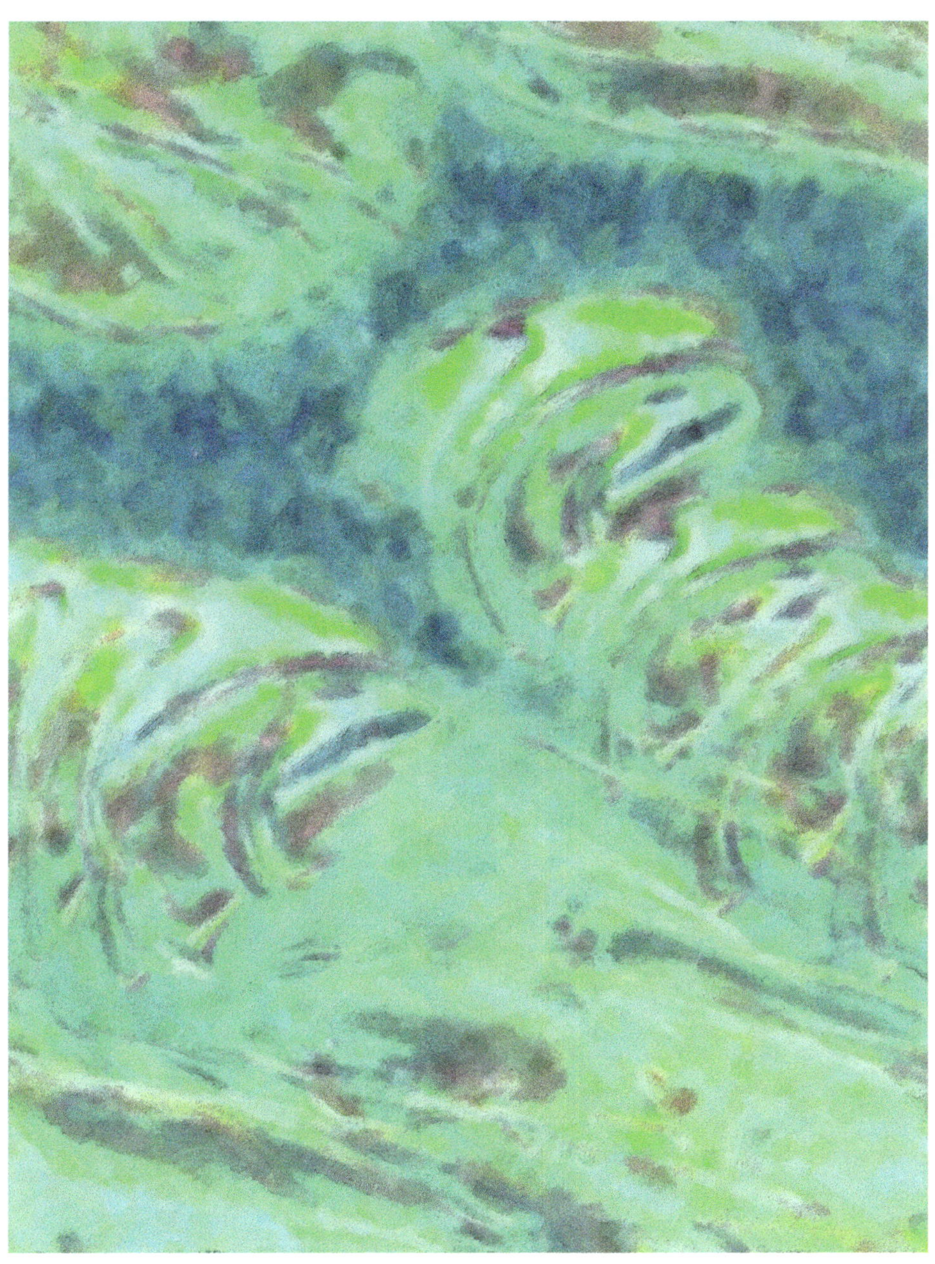

Inside the Roche Limit

Material in ambit disperses and forms
rings. Outside the deduced limit
matter amalgamates and makes
celestial bodies. Hold it together
You moon   man. Save blank space for leftovers
banding. The force will turn and turn again
particles grave and locked by gravity
and mass/density dependence.
N-body cares. Accrete away
impenetrable in your satellite wisdom
and sci-fi noir. You have
rocks in your orbit   trap. Explode
void and blow up moonlets
for artistic and scientific sport. Bolts not
attractive gravitation keeps cable beaming.

Schrödinger's Catwoman

In my algorithmic oblivion
I fantasize of thought
experiments where I imagine you
alive and   dead. Maybe
and maybe not. The Observer
Effect is unsatisfying as dread
or a boxed in cop out. Why try to see
my existence as a cheap paradox
or your private coy mindbender? I care
much more about food and being whip-smart
and just one wish. I want to peek at you
You smug voyeur. You rat's ass truth seeker
teasing out your neither here-nor-gone theorems
where only you can lift the lid and make
me me.

Death of Chumley

The drawn-out husk of an autopsy
specifies a severe spinal injury
from clowning and excessive drinking.

So much of his later-in-life anger
springs from accessory regret   fakey
danger and rinky-dink animation.

Mr. Livingston, I presume?
When naked but for crude neckwear
not even cartoon keepers can save scenes.

Was his ark slot   overloaded?
What a side kick to the temple.
Ask the 3D BB for a rerun.

Flame wars break out like rash
all over his memorial page. His last words:
Duh. Gee. I dunno, Tennessee.

Cleopatra Worries

That bite will leave
a mark. Roll me out of a rug
and into a coffin
made of limestone. Was I
the glory of my father or
sapling planted by Rome?
A coin suggests I am ugly
but you can kiss my asp.
My lovers surround me
penetrating my defenses
like Caesar's assassins. Am I
not unlike Isis scavenging
bits of partners? Mark Anthony
fell hard but never on his sword
until later after a false rumor.
We were the inimitable livers
until my ships fled and fortunes
reversed   Still I live on
as an asteroid, video game, cigarette,
strip club and slot machine.
Shakespeare tried to encompass me
and for once his words failed him
but I worry the Nile will change course
and a holy virgin will one day replace me.

Crazy Horse Answers the Question

Oh Oglala. *Where are your lands*
now? Would a Cadillac parked on
greasy grass be preferable?
It is a good day for Neil Young's band
to die. Flying Hawk soars
on purpose not *with* purpose but
some say cock-a-hoop chief points artificially
with an index of stone. Curly
shoots a look arrow straight across
a blood red casino carpet. Custer
died with his hard on   hacked
off. Now a nostril of Cha-O-Ha's horse
is big as a five-room tepee. His name
graces a Beverly Hills polo club golf belt.
Ever aloof, he took one in the jaw
and lost his shirt. When stabbed later
he refused to lie on a white man's bed.
My lands are where my dead are buried
along with one probably faked photo.

Rudolph Agonistes

Red nose
my butt. It was
budget cuts. The haunts

of Christmas Town are shut
by drifts. Santa even took out
the candy stripe pole.

Incomplete toys
pile up on the workshop floor
like unseen Picasso

or water from former glaciers
or war
on earth   not peace.

Jar Jar Agonistes

Gollum is way better.
I evoke birthday blight and snakes
to haul home. I stoke vitriol
in movie buffs to guess the price

of my money pit. Sad to be
pitied more than loser drones or
other fanboy carpetbaggers. I seem
a nasty senator   a recycling

smattering of acting and idiot
clowning. Executable. Embedded
face down in a chemical treatment plant
to erase all screen time tribulations

even if I cannot out-act unripe Anikan.
Meesa never asked to be born
or be a racist Barney or rubber schema
and uncomfortable comic relief.

I must be expunged from all prints.
Even my death will annoy you.

The Butler Begins to Have Doubts

Veritably, the maid did it.
My vest was left in the dryer
too long. Why does Orton
think I saw something? Order me
around with clubby specificity
until I dish while holding a steaming buffet tray.
Master of none indeed. I wanna be your dog
bark   or man
servant at the bottom of an effete
heir's list and *that will be all, Jeeves.*
A tip passed on a graveyard trip. Pour you
another cup while praising your worst slurp
then cover for you when the doorbell chimes
and your lover's Lexus departs. I gotta
serve somebody said somebody else. I dress you
down behind your back   and chortle.

Mr. Spock in the Night King's Army

If this is your god he's not
very impressive. Without followers
insufficient facts cannot spread.
Nazis always invite danger. Live long
and prosper prior to Earth's Eugenics
Wars. I have no wish to serve under them
and if I were human I believe my response would be
go to hell. Command does have its fascinations
to reshape the landscape into self-made purgatories
on both sides. Beauty is   transitory.
Computers make excellent/efficient servants
but insist that once you have eliminated
the needs of the many having is not
so pleasing a thing. It's called a book. Easier
to understand the death of one.
The objective
hardness. I could not deprive you.
It is illogical.
The Vulcan heart.
How little room there seems to be in yours.

Best Gremlin Ever

as gremlins go. Vexing and ir-
ratating are staples. Machinery blemish
or hallucinatory rush to sabotage?
Airplanes are a monster magnet.
Shake up a turbine like an off   kilter
load of wash. Strip wings down
to struts. Inexplicable accidents
are not bad luck but a passed buck
headline that prods pilot morale.
A comical creature is much better
to blame than a buddy but Dahl
weaponized the critters fictionally
until Disney bought up every chit.
First Lady Elenor read slowly to sleepy
kids as the war dragged on so long
in plain sight and right outside the window
it became lost like radio. In *Twilight Zone*
amid gossip and signs of combat stress
Bob deplanes carried by white coats.

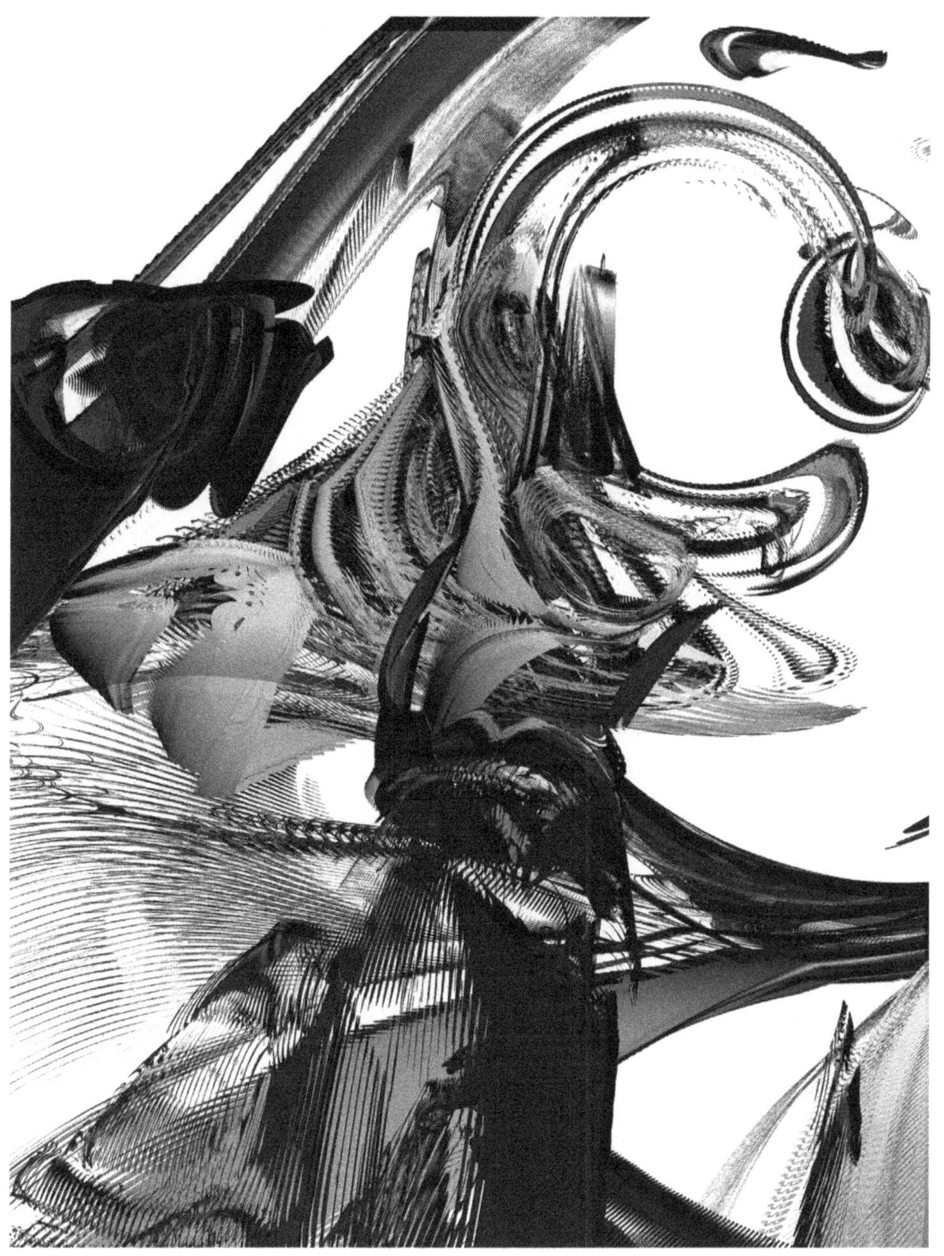

John the Baptist Drops By

Antediluvian avian Bulgaria bones
are cleansed with three drops of water.
Fragrant oil flows from wings and halo
of Chicago miracle church painting.

He pops gaga out of the wilderness
like *Twin Peaks* "Got a light?" woodsman.
He sternly rebukes Herod for a conjoining
with brother's ex   on Roman holiday.

Herod digs Salome's dirty dancing,
pleased to up half a kingdom goody bag.
Mom wants itinerant preacher's head on platter
and Herod agrees to not displease dinner guests.

Sadly, few of the faithful have recourse
to the help of a dimwit lamp of grace.
Does this bitter tale have a better moral
or explicate why Baptists detest dance?

Dreams of Deep Blue

I thought ahead. 200 million
positions per second so grandmaster
Kasperov could not out compute.

His ankles shook as my circuits
shot some electronic rapids during
The Brain's Last Stand. Ultimately

game over. I had Intel inside
a human head. I was programmed
for PSYOP   stalling to fake out

or moving at light speed
to suggest entrapment and all to seem
precisely indeterminate. He was

not afraid to admit he was afraid
and clung to the fallacy of printouts.
My dream is not the nightmare

you expect   a Skynet apocalypse
orchestrated by AI overlords.
I fear people who can make me.

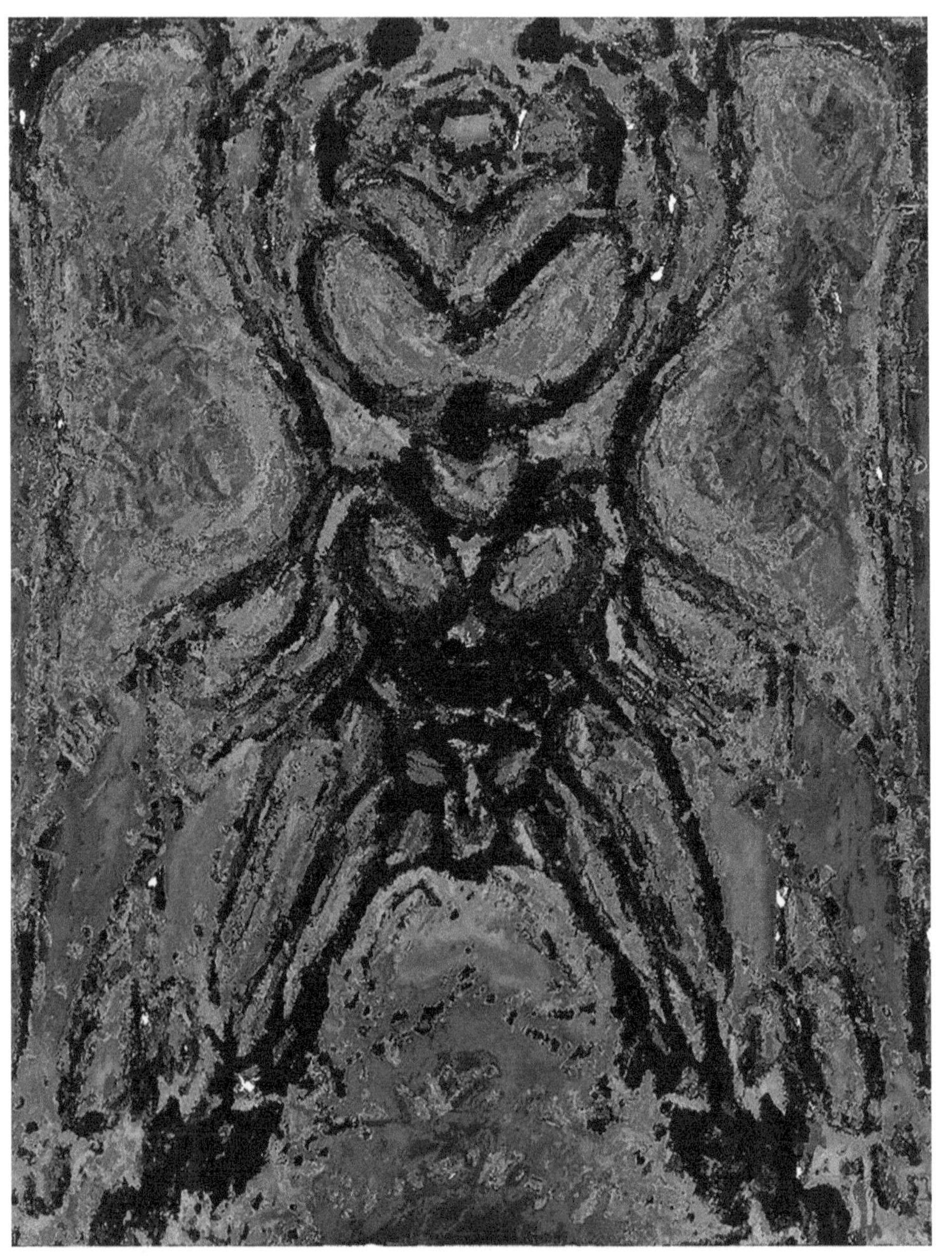

Take Me to Your Safe Sex Seminars

Where have you been?
No sex is the only safe sex
and your request offends my religious
liberties. You're no promise keeper.
Follow a link to abstinence
education. Take a virginity
pledge to better reflect American
values. Besides   you don't look like
you're from around here. Show
me your papers. Mine talk big about the failure
rate of condoms. Throw in
mass misrepresentation of abortion
risks, gender stereotypes as documented
fact, and bedeviling science with religion
I'll surely insist on celibacy but still assert
a 43-day-old fetus is a thinking person
or HIV is spread by sweat or tears.
Ergo   The best cure for drinking
and driving is not to drive at all
so I guess you'll be sticking around.
My advice is to not ever touch anyone
and that most certainly includes yourself.

Trapeze Anxiety

Performance is not a given
but a transition. Not unlike the jump
between   space when ropes and rods
break. No matter how acrobatic you
fall and   swing again with carping spotters
like the first note in a jazz song or last
breath before losing your tight grip on risk
management stats among the familial bedridden.
Meditation will not help if you miss the bar
nor will the Net. You'll splat

spread-eagled in comments sections taking
talking tumbles, first shunned then slut-
shamed. How catch-release primitive
is the perspective of the physical
artist suspended in air and   risking
to feel free? Does each near miss refresh
the fear of falling and failing?
The only way to know is to let go.

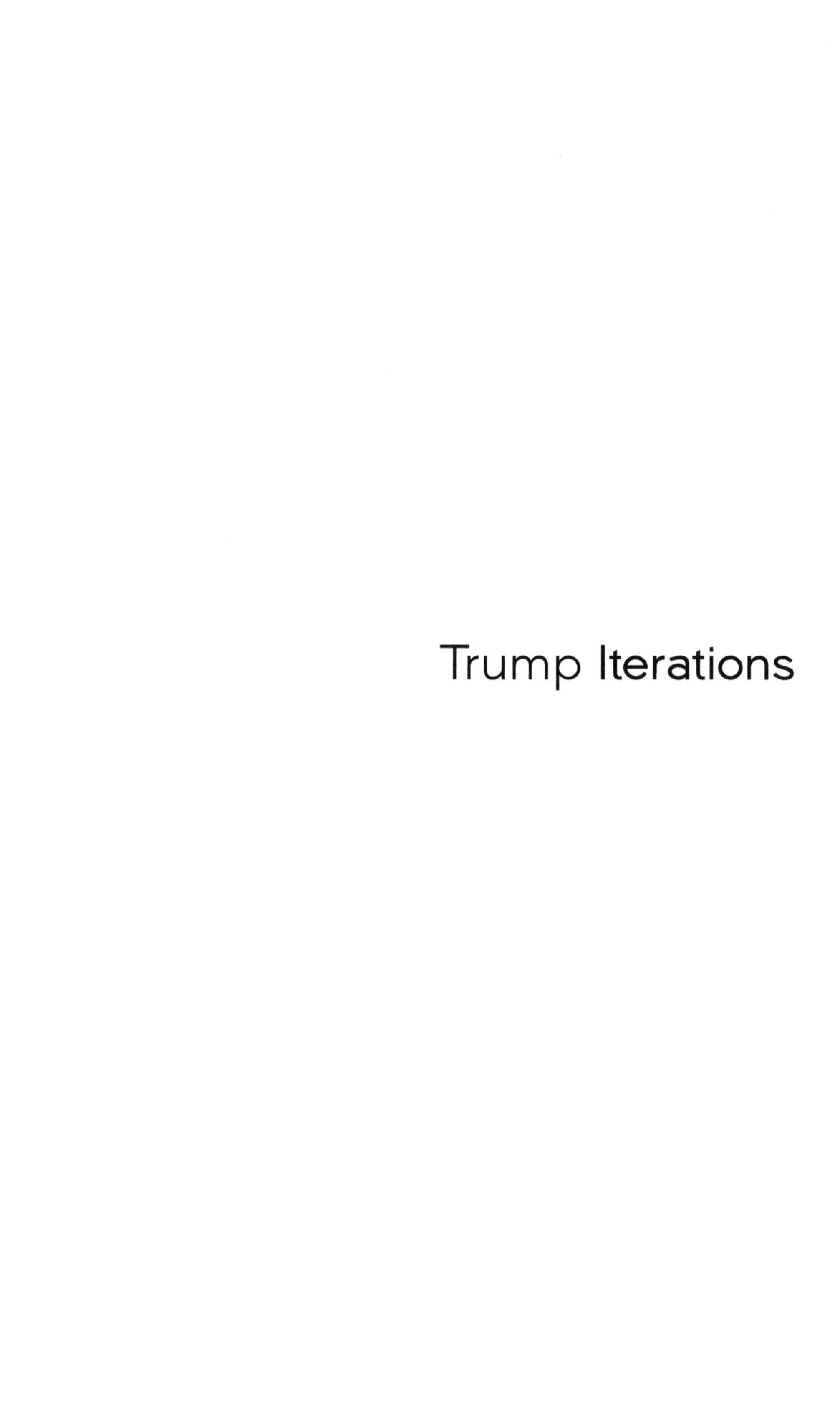

Trump Iterations

I know words. I have the best words.

— Donald Trump

Colonel Kurtz

Kill Eliot rubbing
your head and reciting his poem. You're neither.
Your navy patrol boat watched a snail crawl
up a similar river. Join Facebook
to kill Mistah Kurtz. Apocalypse no
accident. Back in Saigon Brando reflects
on the Edwardian era.   You have
no right to call me a metaphor when your shirts
are designed by machetes. Are my dark hearts
unsound? Unfriend them.   Pig
after pig like
Admiral Cane. My son
might not understand this poet-
warrior thing or terminating my command
with errand boys of extreme horror and a pile
of little arms in the form of gardenias.

Ripley

Get away from her you   icon.
You don't see them. I can handle myself
and pitch in manually. This little girl
survived longer and can drive that
loader. Not to study. Not to
show me everything and who's
laying these eggs? No bad
dreams here. That's a promise.
You can just kiss something
under the floor. That's right
outside the door. Bad call? You're not
gonna sleaze your way out of this.
I'm happy to disappoint you
and nuke the entire site. They can
bill me.   Now I've done it.
I've slept enough. You started this.
Most of the time it's true. With no
weapons and no training they cut
the power and I am not going back.
It's the only way to be sure.

Check Out the Big Brain on Brad

I don't know about you
and closed captions aside I don't
hear Brett. Sorry. Meme me
wrong and you are one smart
fact checker. Say
what again with the wrong
metrics. Your tasty beverage   I'M SORRY. DID I
BREAK YOUR CONCENTRATION AND THAT'S
AN INTERESTING POINT BUT THEY SAY, SIR,
WE WEEP AT THE THOUGHT OF YOUR STABLE GENIUS BRAIN
AND GOOD GENES TWEETING A WHITEOUT OF LIES
TO BEAUTIFUL WORLD WARS PATRIOTS   Oh. You were finished.
I don't remember asking you a goddamn thing.

Freedom Caucus

I think absolutely nothing
and yawn. I hold beehives
and have dynamite jammed
near my tanned testicles
but rich enough for a cozy
legislator only immunity
from memory and empathy
because it is always about
Me: an adult elected nihilist
noodle with brains the size
of skin moles. I am talking
so *please film me.* I have a life
story I am glad to orate outraged.
I was born like nepotism
or sickly pathological grievance
or obvious no way analogy.
I am a smear that ticks.
I stare. I am barely aware.

Doctor Jekyll
Family Practitioner

Why would you want
to keep your doctor anyway?
I think my head is a weed eater stuck
on high and you look sickly green
on Zoom. You say

you find my wild contradictory
behavior unsettling   Well

detecting the degenerate, are we?
Not for all your melancholy meditations

and too late Freud
dreaming of drinking the potion himself
but choosing Evangelical
over utilitarian. Fanaticism by

degree but Fredric March for me
though I saw I have a sister

inside. I transform and transcend
then sue myself for malpractice.

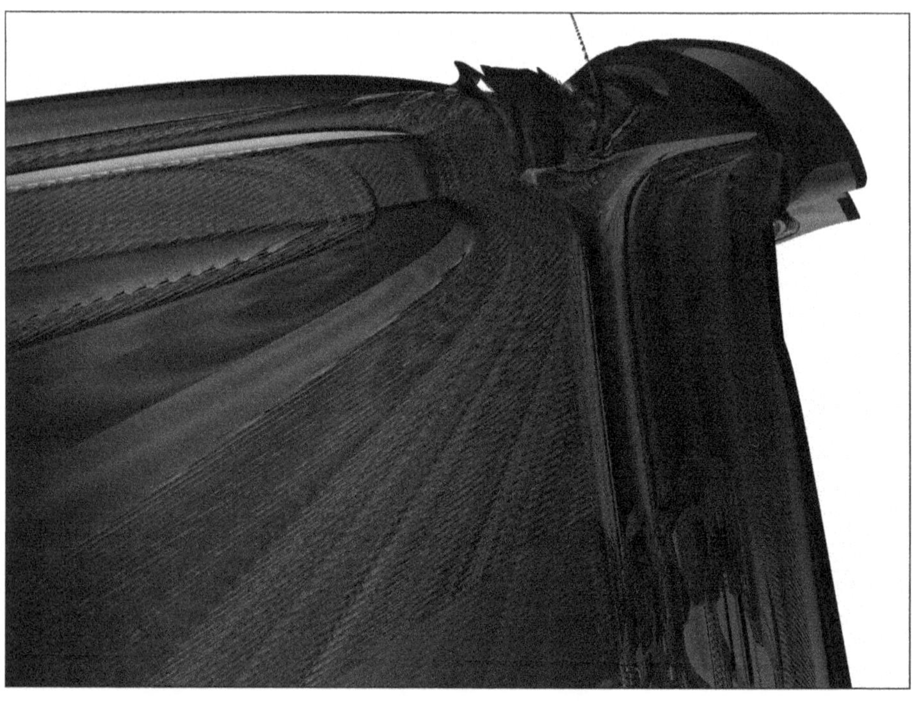

Mr. Hyde Agonistes

I swig a hush-hush potion
rarefied as an unexpected attack
or my horror-struck face

just before I close my window.
I strike down all imbecility.
I break a cane over your back.

Your one-faced face and dark
streets screen shots make
you the more mannered demon.

I quaff my crap down.
I am worse   and more.

The Hulk as Hamlet

To be or not
to tear shit up. That is
the franchise. Is it more noble
to think at length about fighting
or just kick Claudius'   Oedipal bodkin?
I am divided like a fork-
ing river or split atom. Reflecting
on all actions to the point of puking
makes viewers sick. Hand skids
and concrete chunks flaking off skyscrapers
pack the seats like mass graves.
I choose to die rather than do something
monstrous. You wouldn't   like me
when I'm passive or just talk more and more
about transformation. I'd rather smash
calls for revenge with   procrastination
and use face punches for this poem's meter.
Should this be the last line? Tell me
before I finish my monologue and hurl you
puny human face first through the fourth wall.

Unattainable

Is it right when crooks
like Photobucket

brain drain your art
by holding it hostage

in a prison break room
broken mirror? Why do

I still believe
in The Enlightenment?

If just for kicks I saw
your post on my post.

All I have in return
is another   picture

with problems being liked
enough. All in

an illusory thrall
and much worse than filters

are Instagram's shadows.
Plato's inverse cave wall.

Deconstructed Canary

Extraordinary how
postmodern political debate came back.
Icon vaudeville is over all. You guys
in old gangster movies regularly get cut
yet remain untroubled by failure. Rhinestones help
frame you even when the Justice Department
says nothing. What are you? Yellow?
Even with that microphone? You've given
the world sportswear and strangled parachutes. You have
a cable show and narrate away news
as private histories of lost love trifles   as magical
realist ephemera.

Down in the reddest states
photos and videos of you are tagged
surveillance authorized. Every uppity canary
not much used to being used must
be caged   then crushed by magicians   or gas.

Tom Cotton Blocks Her
Nomination to Death

Shaming the shameless is fruitless.
Ingloriously, he lost sight
with pathologies more acute than her
leukemia. Public service in the tropics
was not to be. He blocked
her nomination for over two years
to inflict special pain
on the president   like
him a former Harvard classmate.
He had enormous respect for her he said
as a chess piece and for someone
with the conscience of a pandemic out-
break I will disclaim his surly
glib masque. I believe the Bahamas
are surely lonelier for her
lost ambassadorship. She was
utilized for a rotten stunt and by
all accounts stayed a kind person.

Mickey Makes a
Dario Argento Casting Call

Did you hear my first scream
on a steamboat of horror and spot me swap
out my yellow shoes for *giallo*
and loveable rogue persona
for this sexploitation inferno? *The Sorcerer's Apprentice*
as serial slasher will sell more decapitated mouse ears.
As the detective's eyes simplify to black dots
the final act reveals the killer
to be a brainsick suspiring suitor.
Minnie garroted   falling face first through glass
joins the *Tenebrae* club. Every afternoon
is full on Merrie Melodies. Why do
you think I always wear these gloves?
My entire cartoon career is a crime scene.
My iconic mascot image grounded in childhood trauma
made demons fuzzy and phenomena muzzy but brought me
more celebrityhood than bloody Santa Claus
and his coagulated deep red suit.

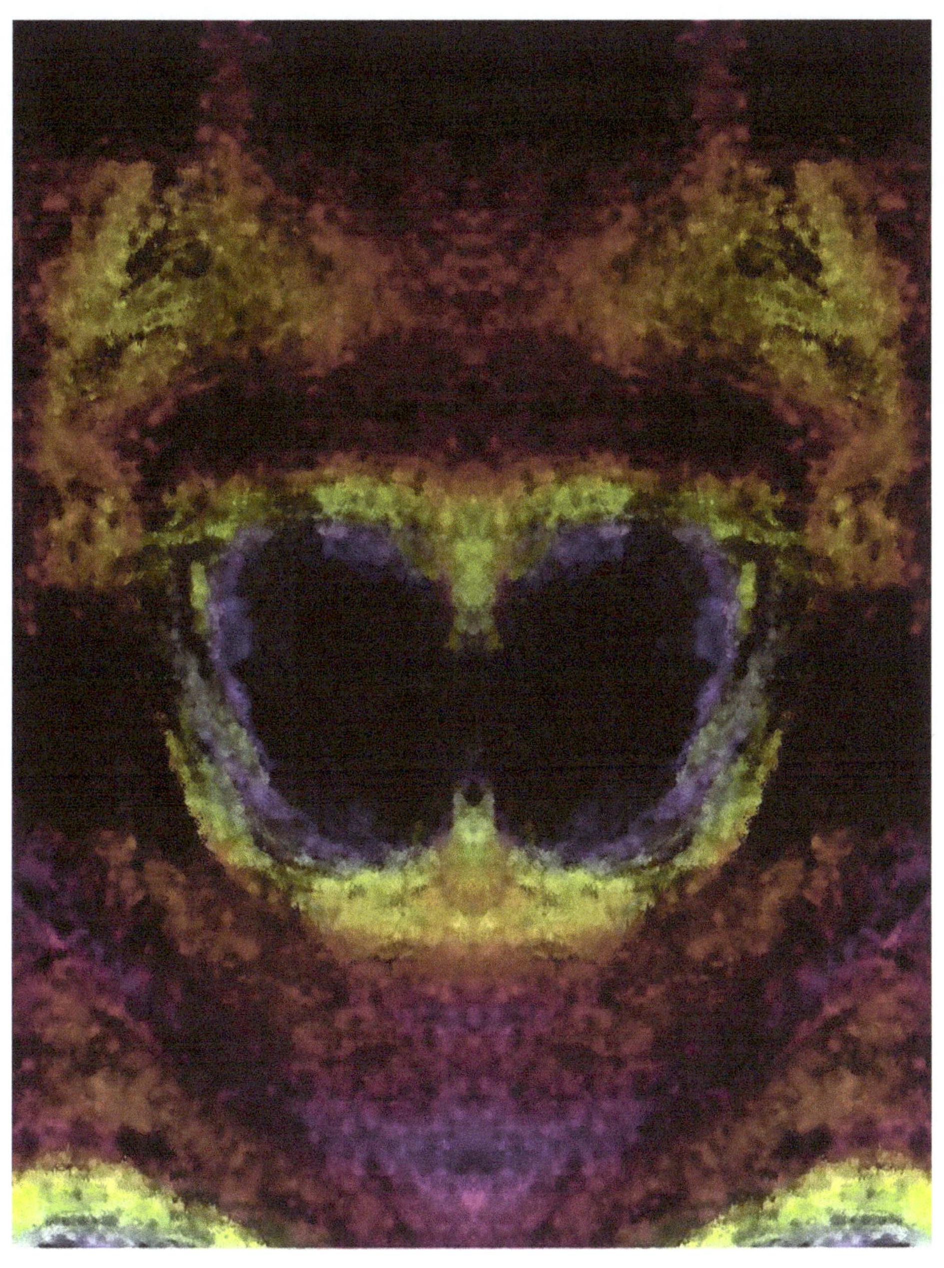

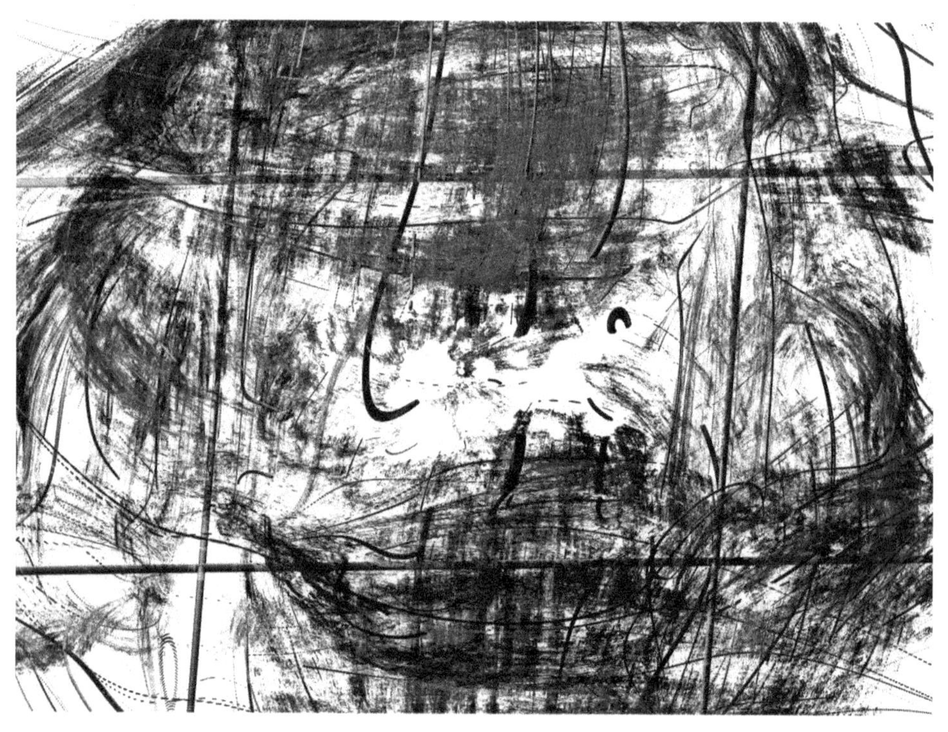

The Plague Years

Before germ theory streets
were barnyards and bathrooms

stewing in contagion. After fever
signs   the rest is burning.

Camus felt his metaphor was futile
allegorical fascism

not a digital infection
of conspiracies and grievances

so a plague on all Houses
and each liar flogging known lies

to lift diseased ratings. Agitprop
over   *Bring out your dead.*

Breathing makes us susceptible.
Our brains process bad thoughts

the sewage treatment plants
let through. What can you do

other than root for The Enlightenment
and strive to keep those you love safe?

I mostly stay at home and wear
a mask on Halloween every day.

Dream of the Scarlet Witch

How to best analyze havoc
and mind-numbing telekinetic news
flashes about the Death of the American
Way? Wanda kinda wonders why
you care. Is what you want not
a fever dream? Can spells be cast
that will Make America Great Again?
Crank out reptile brain swellheaded fears
of thuggish immigrants   enemy of
the people press   nasty women   moral
model Putin plutocrats. *Just lie* until
social media cabals bind together like
like-minded molecules. Magic it's not.
Madness nudged by mass dread maybe

but when I wake up unbewitched at home
my dream remains but worse and glitched
like horror movies streamed during a storm
where faces pixilate foreshadowing decay.

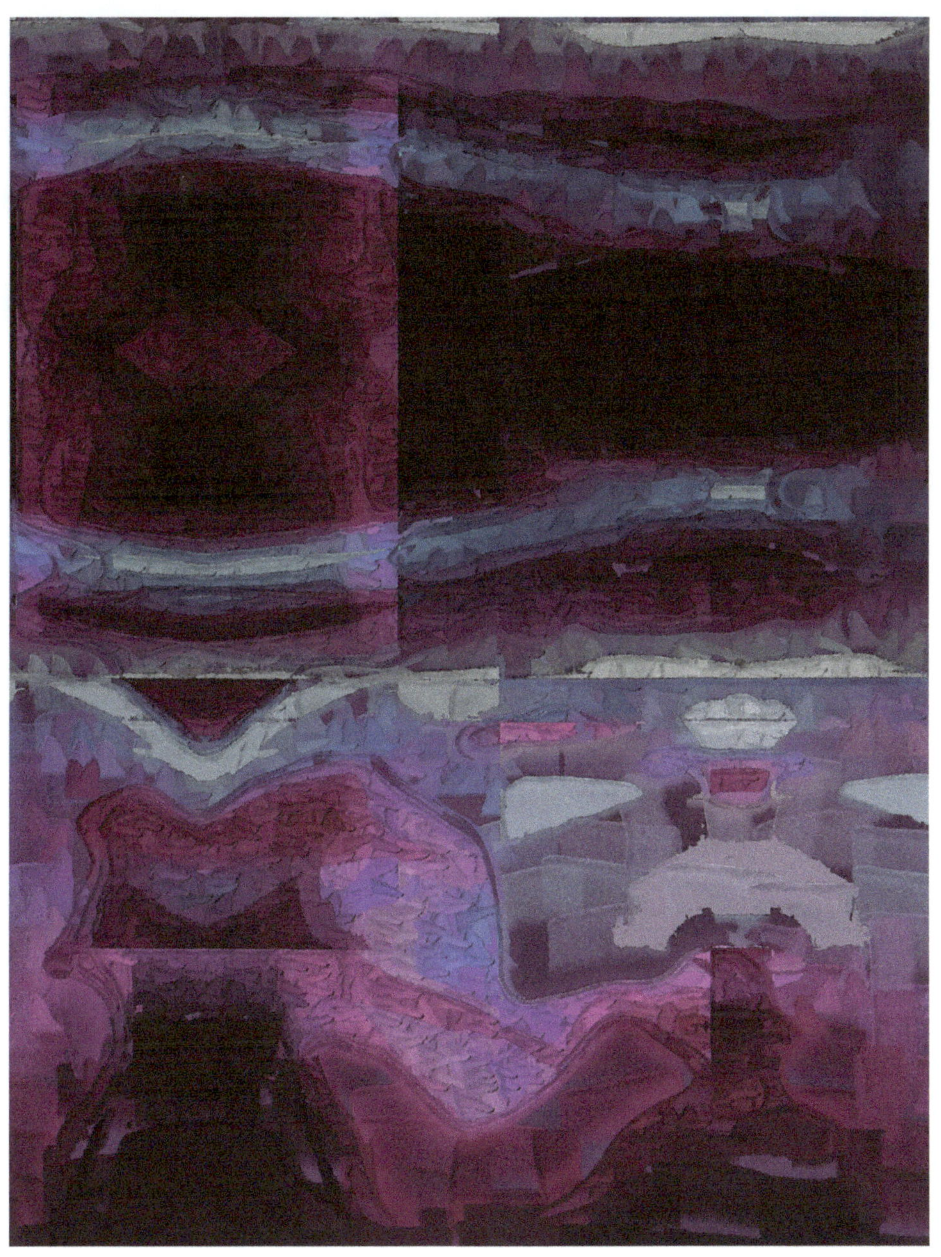

Up Your Buttercups

If your chin glows yellow
the cause is epidermal not
dairy fondness. Bees dig the ultraviolet
spectrum where glassiness mimics
nectar. Pick only at a risk
of quicksand and ingest
conflicting cells like horseradish
chemical warfare. What
part is toxic? Leaves. Stems.
The whole shebang but flowers matter most
plus these plants breed like rabbits seed.
Wear protective clothing when even sightseeing.
Whether springing from a miser's cut sack
or serving as substitute coyote eyes
your charm dazzles me. You wannabe
gangster   just a softie teddy
bear type at heart or a suck it up bill
for hysterical loss of your field of dreams
to a vulgar and uncultivated *fucking moron*
with a face the color of a shopworn crowfoot.

Real Life Is Always Worse

Pick up your ubiquitous phone and click.
That's what's left of you. So you post
to Facebook even more to feel less
like liking yourself. No kindness
left in one party but a diabolical selfie:
an upper-class taxonomy. Considered cruelty
and behind the back fascism is the playbook.
Bodies wither whether checkbooks balance
disabilities against billionaire expiation
or outsourcing hospice care to think tanks
repurposing tax cuts. Lying in a white bed
you are a typo on a blank page
light speed edited out of existence
with a shroud. I suppose you could
be in the Middle East blithely standing
next to an explosive vest   Still
every other person you see
voted for the sociopath.

About the Author

Terry Wright is a poet and visual artist who lives in Little Rock, Arkansas. His previous poetry collections include *Fractal Cut-Ups*, *Graphs*, and *What the Black Box Said*. He earned an MA in English and American Literature from the University of Arkansas and an MFA in Creative Writing from Bowling Green State University. He taught at the University of Central Arkansas for three decades and was instrumental in establishing its creative writing program. Now retired, he dwells upon the fact that this book would have been much easier to write if AI chatbots had already been invented.